In Times Like These ...

A Memoir

Diane Krentel Hodge

Ampelos Press

In Times Like These . . . A Memoir
© 2020 by Diane Krentel Hodge
ISBN: 978-0-9821653-7-9

Published by Ampelos Press, 951 Anders Road, Lansdale, PA 19446
https://writehisanswer.com/Ampelospressbooks, mbagnull@aol.com.

Cover photo by Nastasya Day from Pexels.

Printed in the United States of America

To my three sons
Brian, Stephen, and Benjamin

My wish today for you is to encourage you
to constantly be looking for "God-Stories" in your life.
Where did you see God's hand at work today?
This book is to help you remember
some very important "God-Stories" in our family
to share with your children and others.
I love you with my whole heart.

Mom

Contents

1 ~ Fifties Gal

Guard your heart above all else,
for it determines the course of your life.
Romans 12:1

I grew up in the fifties. One girl surrounded by three brothers. I had to learn how to climb a tree faster, hit back when necessary, and outperform my brothers in order to survive. One of six children, right in the middle, taking root in modern day suburbia.

Back then, children rode their bikes to school, ran barefoot all summer, and played outdoors—all around the neighborhood—right until the fireflies came out. It was an innocent, carefree time to grow up.

I was a regular plain Jane adorned with short straight bangs and two neat braids. I embraced life with great enthusiasm and questioned very little. I was like a straight arrow—never missing church and rigorously following the teachings, instruction, and models I was exposed to. I asked Jesus to come into my life at my mother's knee when I was five years old after attending many Bible clubs and Sunday school sessions.

When anyone asked me what I wanted to be when I grew up, I would say with great pride, "A mom with five kids!" You know, I think most gals back then had grandeur dreams of homemaking. Endless hours each day were spent playing kitchen with plastic pots and pans, caring for baby dolls that cried real tears and wet diapers, or dressing up for a romantic ball with "Prince Charming." If you really were well off and spoiled, you might even have had your very own playhouse in the backyard, with real windows and doors . . . a place all your own to act out your dreams of homemaking.

And who can say how much a new invention called the television impacted my young mind? I remember with awe the day the box was delivered to our small ranch in North Carolina. We were totally captivated and sat down right in front of the screen taking in the magic. It was an era after the war which focused on the family with shows like *Leave It to Beaver* and *Life with Father*. Warm.

Inviting. An innocent world with little violence, immorality, and heartaches.

Besides these inspiring role models and dreams of getting married when I grew up, the only other professions girls dreamt of back then seemed to fall into two areas . . . the careers of nursing or teaching. The local library opened up a window into these careers for little girls as well.

Back then, the public library was a focal part of the community and sometimes right in your own neighborhood where it was easy enough to walk to after school. Each week you could select six special books to take home that counterbalanced your daily intake of television and play.

Girls especially gravitated toward those light blue mystery books, the Nancy Drew series, and the fiction books with bright red covers, the Cherry Aims nurse series. Nursing became more viable as a career with each new red book I delved into. Soon I was setting my "dream sails" and tacking in that direction as well. For me, teaching was less glamorous, as the popular TV series, *Our Miss Brooks,* didn't really inspire me to follow in her steps. Instead, I fancied myself dressed in a perfectly starched white uniform with a beautiful white coifed hat resting on my curly teased hairdo. I'd look glamorous with no braces, short bangs, or pimples that desperately needed the miraculous pasty Clearasil®.

In the fifties, there always was the exception to this career rule—the "horn-rimmed glasses" gal in your class. She was the unpopular one who reached for the outer limits, sat up front in class, and desired to become a doctor or perhaps even a lawyer! But for most average girls, there were only three choices in the fifties, plain and simple— being a homemaker, nurse, or teacher. Boy, have times changed!

Life has a way of tinting your naive experiences with a strong dose of reality. Soon my outlook of innocence was shaken to the core.

One day at school in eighth grade, I was summoned to the office where a friendly neighbor greeted me and drove me home. I was given no reason for this early dismissal, but I was not worried at all. But when I opened the front door of our ranch house, I soon realized that life can take a turn that can't be erased or rationalized. I stepped over the threshold into a heartrending situation that imprinted on my mind forever.

Martha, my five-month-old, perfectly created sister, had died this beautiful sunny day. Our family was jettisoned into a world of grief. Aching arms stayed sadly empty. Hearts split wide open. Tears flowed. Conversations went on way into the wee hours of the morning. Crib death was the diagnosis, but it all didn't make sense to me.

At the funeral, I remember vividly how I leaned down to Martha's small casket to kiss her goodbye. For the first time I experienced the coldness of death. I was an impressionable thirteen-year-old. Plainly she was gone, and I was shaken deep into my inner being.

I honestly can say that my mother and father bravely faced this horrible happening with the faith I had witnessed all my life. Their deep-down faith was that nothing could separate us from God's love: death can't, life can't, angels can't, demons can't, fears for today can't, worries for tomorrow can't, powers of hell can't (Romans 8:38). Nothing in creation can.

Mother and I slowly packed up the nursery together, all but one pink and blue blanket, Martha's favorite. Each piece of clothing was thoroughly smelled and hugged before we closed the trunk and wiped each other's tears. This Martha-lesson threw me into the trenches of life and colored how I would go through other tragedies. These were formative years that seemingly didn't fit in with those innocent dreams I set when younger.

Then two years later, my second sister, Melissa was born. At first, we were all so excited as this baby would be loved doubly. Our arms just wanted to hold a baby once more. I was fifteen then and reveled in the new birth. But life had another lesson for me go through . . . one more baby to mourn for . . . another advanced course in life to learn from.

Happiness vanished as we gradually learned that Melissa had a condition called Down syndrome. Back then we knew little about this condition, but soon the doctors painted a clear picture of what Melissa's life would probably be like. Once again, I witnessed my parents' resolve and faith as they waded through all the decisions they faced.

Our family had to maneuver through the painstaking trial of placing our treasure into a home for special children faraway in Ohio. No trip home from the hospital for Melissa. My brothers and I stood in the driveway to say our sad farewells because if we held her or brought her inside . . . well, we just didn't trust ourselves. So, we all watched her drive away with Mom and Dad for distant Ohio. For you see, doctors, pastors, and friends all strongly advised us this was the right thing to do, given that there were four teenagers in the household. These "experts" and concerned friends underscored the negative affect of bringing a special needs child into a family, predicting that the whole family would focus around her like cogs of a wheel. Dutifully, we obeyed and numbly implemented their advice.

A few weeks after, it was time for Mother and me to pack up the trunk of all the bits and pieces of what was going to be Melissa's nursery. Our hearts literally ached once more. A second nursery put away, and it didn't get any easier the second time around.

However, the story doesn't end here. After several months, we drove to Ohio to bring Melissa home for Christmas. You probably can guess the rest. We ignored all the advice of the "learned" and kept her all to ourselves! We didn't care if she had one more or one less chromosome. We almost felt like happy thieves as we watched her acclimate to her new surroundings in our home. Those months were completely joyful as our love was requited finally.

This second Melissa-test also led my parents to dream a rather life-changing dream. As they had looked for a special place for Melissa to live in the beginning, they had seen many unhappy institutions for little ones with handicaps like Melissa. This bleak realization soon grew in their minds, and they were determined to provide better care than what they had witnessed for children like Melissa. With God's help, they were determined to succeed! So, they started a home called Melmark for Melissa—Mel for Melissa, Mar for Martha, and K for Krentel.

The whole family was united in what this would mean to us. We indeed began to focus around Melissa and others like her, just like the experts had foretold. Like cogs in a wheel. I watched as my parents threw themselves into this project 200% . . . selling our family home, taking other children into our family, writing two books all about this opportunity for service (*Melissa Comes Home* and *Melmark the Home that Love Built*), networking with other charities, fund-raising, Dad giving up his job, inviting staff to live with us like new brothers and sisters, buying a mansion for the children to live in . . . There were countless changes. But this is another whole story.

By this time, I was seventeen years old. Childhood has a way of tiptoeing by quickly in spite of rather large happenings like these.

College years were here before I knew it. With great anticipatory zeal, I set my cap to live out the world of my old dreams. I packed my suitcase and trunk, making sure I had plenty of knee-highs, miniskirts, tease combs, hair spray, my trusty girdle, and seamed stockings. Facing the world I created in my mind, I was innocently determined it would be just perfect. After all, I had great faith.

It didn't take long for me to realize that this new journey was in an arena much different than what I had imagined. The luggage I brought with me was not only the physical suitcases, packed to the brim, but a prior knowledge of life's experiences that formed the scaffolding of who I was and how I would make decisions and face the ups and downs of life. For me, reality didn't always match up with the fantasy world I had believed in that was so right, so fair, so exciting, and so full of those things that I thought "ought-to-be" or "should-have-been." Rather it would soon take me into a voyage that no TV program or book would ever be tempted to glamorize. This journey of life was richer, engulfing not only the happy experiences of life but those life happenings that dig down deeply into your spiritual reserve and "the garden of your soul," the seeds of which often are sown in those first innocent years of life.

2 ~ College Days

You saw me before I was born.
Every day of my life was recorded in your book.
Every moment was laid out
before a single day had passed.
Psalm 139:16 NLT

I n reality, I don't think anyone is ready for college. Separation from the secure nest of childhood and facing independence for the first time, shakes all you know of life to date. Higher education can be thought of as the first arena where you test how well your foundation stands up and supports you. This college journey would take me on a trek into an unknown theater where challenges and struggles caused me to draw deep from the reservoir within.

I joined the student body of a small Methodist conservative college called Houghton. I remember the trip to Houghton like it was just yesterday. Mom and Dad sat in the front seat in their best Sunday "go-to-meeting" clothes. I sat resolutely in the backseat in my brand-new college suit trying to enjoy the seven-hour trip with no brothers to pinch me or bother me. The car ride itself became a "mini crash course on life" as Mom and Dad fit in last minute instructions on what to do and what not to do in college. This made me have even more fears than I had before.

Everyone was on edge, and if that wasn't enough, immediately upon arrival on campus a freshman beanie was squashed on my head, crushing my new perm. I was thrown into a world of confusion as I faced a mirage of required orientation procedures . . . planning my semester roster, finding my combination mailbox, buying my books, meeting my new roommate, and unpacking—just to name a few. Each task included long lines to test my patience and increase the fear that I would be closed out of a class before even getting up to the check-in table.

Navigating through all these experiences can be a daunting feat even for the most mature freshman. As for me, this initiation was shocking as there was no special college weekend to welcome you or candlelight service of dedication to get you started with encouraging thoughts. Instead, it was like being thrown into a cold pool, not knowing how to swim. Interestingly enough, throughout these adjusting times in this new world of academia, I noticed my focus was no longer on whether my "flip" hairdo looked cool or whether or not there was a "hunk" in my scheduled classes. Rather it was centered solely on staying afloat and learning how I was supposed to succeed in this new mental arena.

After surviving the first day, going to classes and learning the new routine became the next feat. I always sat in the front seat of most classrooms, that is, if I found the classroom! I thought sitting in the front would make me appear eager and up for the challenge. But soon I realized that positioning myself under the nose of every austere professor was another upheaval for my sensitive insides.

The professors had a way of making you feel you knew nothing at all, and they spoke a most different language devoid of all the "cool, blast, and neat" vernacular of my childhood era. Suddenly this slang became passé, and I was confronted with the dire need of using my Webster as one would use a Bible. To make matters worse, it soon became apparent that my college prep courses in high school failed miserably to reflect the scholastic requirements I faced in this college.

One clear recollection of this was in my Principles of Writing class. I had the same English professor as my parents did when they attended the college many years back. She stood before us with black laced-up shoes, a pure white bun stacked on her head, and rimless spectacles perched on her nose. Of course, she smelled of lavender. Dr. Joe rarely smiled, and her dresses draped down to her ankles. I quickly tugged at my short skirt. As I crossed the threshold of her classroom, my inner confidence continued to wane.

Our first assignment was to write a descriptive piece about the autumn season. We were dismissed and told to go out in the woods, observe, and write down at least 1,000 words to describe what we saw. Only a couple of pages were required, but it was to be filled with all the eloquence we could muster up!

Soon I found myself sitting in damp leaves, looking around at the drooping forest, and floundering in fear. I had no "epiphany moment" trudging through this laborious process. I passed in my piece on time and it was promptly returned with red marks everywhere. D- stood out for all to see. My spirits were dashed. No honor roll for me this semester. My first taste of reality.

Another factor to adjust to was what I will call the "dating-factor" at Houghton. Gradually I realized that the boy to girl ratio was so bad, you could almost go a few days without seeing a single male on campus! If I had wanted to go to a girl's school, I would have done so. This situation was not optimum for me, I thought immaturely.

Thankfully, I had a great roommate. Marcia, a farmer's daughter who enjoyed a good laugh, was graced with intelligence and beauty. We were on the same wavelength. On date nights we would hang out the window over the front door of the dorm and spy on other gals getting their goodnight kisses. Frankly, we spent a lot of time laughing about this "island" experience called "college life." One exam night we even construed a "best ten men" list just for fun and went out to see if we could get them to even say hello to us!

To make the dating factor even worse, there was only one phone per floor in the four-story antiquated dorm. Can you imagine only four phones per three hundred talkative girls? This phone was a constant reminder of the lucky girls who got called to go out on dates! And guess who was assigned the room right across from the only phone on our floor? Yes, Marcia and I were the select ones to hear it ring about every five minutes. Whoever was closest was supposed to pick it up and loudly announce the lucky girl's name who was getting a phone call for a date.

What delight! Of course, with each annoying ring, it became apparent that we weren't in great demand. No one had put us on their list, it seemed.

It didn't take long to figure out who the popular ones were going to be. And by October, Marcia and I were dismayed and disillusioned about the "boy-factor." Our preconceptions about beauty and our fetching persona were deeply shaken.

Contrary to today's youth, who start their evening activities around 10:00 p.m. and stay up all hours of the night, at our college, you had to be back in your room each night promptly at 10:30 p.m. To add misery to heartache, there was also a regular bed check to confirm your presence, safe and sound. No need to miss your mom here!

There also was a strict dress code that prohibited girls from showing their shoulders or kneecaps. Regardless, I would rebelliously roll up the waistline of all my skirts under my bulky sweaters just to make them shorter and more in vogue. Miniskirts were "in" back then in the real world. For the life of me, I could never figure out why these body areas were too exciting anyhow, and I felt such rules just made these areas all the more fetching.

It wasn't long after taking this all in that I reasoned, "Why, oh why, had I chosen this college, and what was I to do?" By October, I was ready to go home, forfeit my first vain goal of being a nurse, and/or change colleges. My parents, sensing a problem, arrived suddenly for a visit the very next weekend.

After long discussions, with a heavy dose of reality checks, we constructed my survival plan. I would change majors from Nursing, which I had discovered was a hefty challenge to me already. Chemistry was the chief culprit! So, since I liked children so much, Elementary Education looked inviting to me now. I also found out El.Ed. was considered less of an academic challenge. Making this change encouraged me to persevere at Houghton for at least two more years. Then we would reevaluate the situation and make changes if necessary. I dropped Chemistry immediately.

Before my parents left campus that important weekend so long ago, I remember how we drove down the hill to a quaint little store called Barkers to shop for some much-needed supplies and a birthday gift for my roommate. What better time to do this then when Dad was there with his wallet to lend a helping hand? This turned out to be the eventful day when I met "Mr. Right," and I didn't even know it!

Ron, a tall and handsome well-dressed upperclassman, waited on us. Suddenly I recognized him as one of the "lucky-ten" on Marcia's and my silly list. Here he was standing right before me. I was dumbfounded and nervous.

As it so happened, at that time there was a contest running at the quaint little country store. November was fast approaching. Anyone who made a purchase would receive a coupon to be cast into a pot for a free turkey. (Now I ask you, what would a college student want a turkey for?) But anyhow, I threw in my ticket with all the others and left with my birthday gift in hand.

No apparent lightning flashes went off about this tall and handsome clerk who waited on me. My parents left and dorm life settled back to a routine in my "not so perfect" picture of college. Making a nip and a tuck adjustment in my course load and a stretch in my thinking to "hold on" for a few more years, I moved on. At the same time, my "inner child" ideas of college life continued to slowly dissolve.

One day while my fingers were slowly pecking out a composition on my new electric typewriter, the phone rang again on our floor. This time I heard loudly, "Diane Krentel, phone for Diane Krentel!" Mercy me!

I ran over to the phone and picked it up. Lo and behold, it was that handsome clerk, Ron. After a short introduction, he stated, "I just wanted to call and tell you the results of the turkey contest at Barkers."

My word I thought . . . *what a strange reason to call.* I was baffled on what to say next. But soon I heard a warm chuckle on the other end of the line, and he rescued me. He assured me he was just joking and asked if I would I like to go to a movie with him next weekend.

And this became our first date . . . a date that started more than a fifty-year relationship where love has ruled each day and held us together for better and worst.

Ron was an intelligent, good-looking, Christian young man. Dates, back then, were comprised of walking for miles under a solitary umbrella (it always was raining at Houghton), going to movies and sharing popcorn, spooning in the dorm lounges, hunting together (believe it or not we shot rats at the dump), and parking "across the river." Soon there would be no more talk of transfer for me! I had found my soul mate in this island experience at this challenging school, Houghton.

Each new feat in college broadened and prepared me more for my walk with God. I suppose if I were to choose the most lasting lesson during this time, it would be the one shared by a woman English professor in my senior year. She was a bit lackluster and not at all attractive, but she was one of those intellectual types who caught your attention. She sourly stated one day, "Many of you are engaged and have no business getting married because you don't know how to be happy all alone." Immaturely, I thought how rude and jealous she must be of all of us who sported new quarter-carat diamonds to class.

I never fully grasped the meaning of this until many years later raising a family when I had to share Ron with the challenges of working for a top-rated global company. I seemed almost to be a spectator some weeks as I watched him climb up the corporate ladder. Many times, I was alone, supporting Ron from the quietness of his home.

I often thought about what that professor said so long ago when spring and love were in the air everywhere. What a gem she gave us to ponder on and refine! I was learning firsthand that as wonderful as Ron was, he still couldn't take the only place in my heart. Who really was the captain of my ship? Who steered it to happiness? I then knew what that professor had tried to tell us back in college.

The happiness that the Lord gives is not the happiness driven by situations, circumstances, or your husband. What that spinster professor was trying to teach us was that our own sense of well-being and peace comes from the fullness of a walk with our Savior through the ho-hum of daily routines, the numbing quiet days, and the uneventful days where we live and breathe.

The following poem exemplifies what she was trying to teach us. Its wisdom is fathomless. The poem has been a favorite to share over the years. Thank you, Houghton, for this pearl and for giving me the man of my dreams.

Be Satisfied with Me

Everyone longs to give themselves
completely to someone,
To have a deep soul relationship with another,
To be loved thoroughly and exclusively.

But God, to a Christian, says,
"No, not until you are satisfied,

*fulfilled and content
with being loved by Me alone,
With giving yourself totally and unreservedly to Me,
With having an intensely personal and unique
relationship with Me alone.*

*Discovering that only in Me
is your satisfaction
to be found,
Will you be capable of
the perfect human relationship
That I have planned for you.
You will never be united with another
until you are united with Me alone,
Exclusive of anyone or anything else,
Exclusive of any other desires or longings.
I want you to stop planning, stop wishing,
And allow Me to give you
the most thrilling plan existing,
One that you cannot imagine.
Please allow Me to bring it to you.*

*You just keep watching Me, expecting the greatest things.
Keep experiencing the satisfaction that I Am.
Keep listening and learning the things I tell you.
You just wait. That's all. Don't be anxious.
Don't worry.
Don't look at the things you think you want;
You just keep looking off and away up to Me,
Or you'll miss what I want to show you.
And then when you are ready,*

I'll surprise you
with a love far more wonderful than any
You could dream of.

You see, until you are ready and until
The one I have for you is ready
(I am working even at this moment to have you both
ready at the same time),
Until you are both satisfied exclusively with Me
And the life I prepared for you,
You won't be able to experience the love that
Exemplified your relationship with Me.
And this is the perfect love.

And dear one, I want you to have
this most wonderful love,
I want you to see in the flesh a picture of your
Relationship with Me,
And to enjoy materially and concretely
The everlasting union of beauty,
perfection and love
That I offer you with Myself.
Know that I love you utterly. I AM God.
Believe it and be satisfied.

St. Anthony of Padua

The girl of my youth changed quickly at college. God was faithful and allowed me to not only find a wonderful partner for life at Houghton and receive a good GPA, but

He allowed me to realize that the key for happiness was directly corresponding to my walk with my Savior. This walk was foundational in facing life's challenges and joys, some that were even more stretching than what I had experienced in college. Marriage became my dream, and I graduated the middle of my Junior year to walk the aisle with my dear Ron.

3 ~ Married Life
A Tapestry Woven

"And the LORD is the one who goes ahead of you;
He will be with you.
He will not fail you or forsake you.
Do not fear, or be dismayed."
Deuteronomy 31:8 NASB

At first married life was pretty much how I had imagined it. To me, it was sheer joy to spend all the time I could with the man of my dreams. The "give and take" of those first few years were effortless, for the most part, due to our deep love for each other. The first burnt meal, shrunk piece of laundry, scorched shirt, and lack of good communication seemed to squeak by with no real lasting negative affect.

Just like my childhood dream, we soon were talking of having that big family I always wanted. In my naiveté, I assumed getting pregnant would go without a hitch, like everything else in our marriage to date. My heart nearly soared from just the thought of being pregnant. I was so eager to be a mom. But it wasn't long when we began to realize that having a family wasn't as effortless as we thought. Our marriage tapestry was being drawn.

One month piled upon another, with no pregnancy. Before we knew it, a year went by. And with this year, monthly tears of disappointment and failure. Months of taking my temperature each morning religiously to catch the "optimum moment," eating the right foods, and reading every fertility book I could get my hands on. The quest became my daily focus and a monumental trial. My "Mother-in-Love," who was a bit of a tease, would jest and try to cheer us up by stating, "Oh, you guys just don't have the recipe!"

Needless to say, we dutifully kept trying, all to no avail. During three years of doctor appointments, charts, fertility pills, negative pregnancy tests, and tearful monthly cycles, I slowly began to let the most cherished hope for a family go.

I was reading Catherine Marshall's "The Prayer of Relinquishment" in her book, *Beyond Our Selves.* My broken heart resonated with these words. Here is an excerpt that I saved in my daily journal:

> *Acceptance says, "I trust the good will, the love of my God. I'll open my arms and my understanding to what He has allowed to come to me. Since I know that He means to make all things work together for good, I consent to this present situation with hope for what the future will bring.*[1]

She went on to say that in this acceptance, the door is left wide open to hope in "God's creative plan." Not resignation but acceptance.

In her book, *Something More,* she shared that the secret is simply this: the Christian life must be lived in the will, not the emotions.

> *We stop fighting the evil or less-than-good circumstances.*
> *With that, resentment goes;*
> *Self pity goes.*

---

[1] Catherine Marshall, *Beyond Ourselves* (New York: McGraw Hill, 1961), 94.

Perspective comes.

We have turned our back on the problem and are looking steadily at God.

We are acting out our belief in the character of God—His goodness, His Love.

We are acting out our belief in the present power of God—in His participating Presence. [2]

It was as if the Lord was trying to get my attention as I read her books. I learned that anything, however good, that I put on a pedestal of my heart as a source of JOY is like an idol. I sensed that He was telling me to take that one thing that is so important, take it off the pedestal, give it all up, and place it in His hands. The Lord wanted me to stop trying to control this situation but rather open my hand, so to speak, and relinquish this infertility to Him—giving up what I had always wanted the most and trusting Him.

As I was learning this Prayer of Relinquishment, I continued going to my doctor. He was a kind old man. He'd pat me on my back and say not to worry. Just go home and keep trying.

During one of my visits, a blood test was drawn which showed my thyroid was low. This would explain somewhat why I was highly irregular. Thyroid pills were prescribed as

---

[2] Catherine Marshall, *Something More* (Grand Rapids, MI: Baker House, 1974), 40-41.

the magical solution to my problem. Dutifully, I took my thyroid pills with a renewed hope that maybe this would be the magical cure. Sure enough, another month and a half went by, and I again stumbled on down to the doctor's office to take another pregnancy test, one more time. And surprisingly, this time the results were different. Finally, I was pregnant!

What utter joy broke out in the Hodge house. We lived in Ron's hometown. All the relatives and church friends rejoiced with us. I was flying so high. My nesting activities included buying red baby furniture, knitting a sweater, and making my own maternity clothes. Everywhere I walked, I would make sure my stomach was pushed way out in front, as I was so proud of my new shape and the life growing inside. No longer would my heart ache each time I saw a pregnant woman or heard a baby cry in public. I was going to be a mother!

My two baby showers were celebrations. Each new outfit I adoringly lay across my bulging stomach, imagining how it would look on my new wee one. My sister-in-law, Ruthie, was pregnant at the same time. We shared maternity stories across the miles. Everything was back on track it seemed. Happiness reigned. We praised the Lord for this miracle.

I recall the winter of my pregnancy was especially long. There was still snow on the ground by the end of April. I couldn't wait until spring. They thought I was to deliver somewhere the end of May. By June, being two weeks late, I decided I waited long enough, and I tried taking castor liver oil. Two and a half hours later, I was definitely in labor and on my way to the hospital. The anticipation was great, and we nearly had to pinch ourselves to believe the day was finally here after such a long time waiting.

When we arrived at the hospital, each little preparation for birth was a happy ritual—even when I put on the lovely hospital gown with matching booties. Soon the baby monitor was attached, and we waited for the pains to become closer together.

After several hours, it became apparent that the baby's heartbeat on the monitor showed some stress, so they wheeled me into the delivery room. Back then, husbands were not allowed in. I was on my own now. The doctor used forceps to help things along, and before too long the doctor announced, "Mrs. Hodge, you have a baby boy!" Matthew, our "gift of God" entered our lives. But almost in the same moment, the doctor whisked the baby away. There was an eerie silence in the room.

Frantically, I asked, "Why isn't the baby crying?" They all were hovering over the baby. I spoke out again more desperately, "What is wrong?"

Soon a rather motherly nurse took one of my hands and just held it firmly as she told me the baby was alive but there was a problem. I knew right then that it must be something serious. The doctor came over and announced that our long-awaited baby had spina bifida, a neurological birth defect. Even with all my experiences of living at Melmark, I asked him to repeat the name as the shock started to settle in.

My mind raced. I thought surely this was something that can be fixed. I asked question after question, furiously trying to take this all in and make sense of it. The doctor explained that the baby needed to go to another hospital to close up part of his spine so they could keep him from contracting meningitis. I barely got to see the baby or even touch him. He was being rushed over for his first surgery as I was wheeled quickly into the recovery room. Ron accompanied the baby to the other hospital in town, so I was all alone.

I will never forget lying on my back, looking at the clock slowly ticking, and listening to the other new mothers in the curtained off areas of the room. Each one was making happy phone calls to her loved ones about her new baby. There was such joy . . . just a curtain away. My only call was an SOS to my parents and to our pastor. I laid there all alone, filled with questions. Numb. Those hours were some of the hardest I have lived through.

It wasn't long before our pastor was at my side. I will never forget his presence at this tender time. Pastor Stady was of a sturdy build, tall, and had these very large hands. He asked me how I was doing. I closed my eyes and stated that I was going to "go away," as the pain was too great.

He grabbed my weak hand in his large strong one. He didn't quote any Scripture to me, but he very firmly said I was going nowhere and that God would help me bear this pain. His assurance came through his hand and into me as I began to hold on mentally and physically.

Later I was transferred to the maternity ward, along with the two other happy moms in the recovery room. When I closed my eyes again in my own private room, I tried to take everything in and rest so that I could get stronger to see my baby. As I rested, I was almost haunted by a tune I sang at a Christian school choir in eighth grade. *"The Lord is my Light and my Salvation . . ."* Every time I closed my eyes, I heard this song from Psalm 27 over and over again in my head reminding me that "The LORD is my light and my salvation; Whom shall I fear?" (Psalm 27:1 NASB).

During the next day or so as Ron ran between two hospitals checking on the baby and supporting me, the song remained in my mind.

On the second day of my recovery, my older brother, David, who was a minister, came in for a visit. In his hand he clutched a new *Living Letters* Bible. He asked me when I felt able, to turn to Psalm 27 and read it—the very same chapter that was comforting me when I rested. Then I knew the Lord was trying to send me a message.

The words reminded me that He was my High Tower . . . a place to run into when the pain was too great. He was the strength of my life during this time and much more. I gloried in this special message to me from the Lord. It still is amazing to me how God uses things in our past . . . songs memorized . . . Scriptures memorized and mediated on . . . all stored away to be drawn upon in times of need.

Three days went rather quickly and soon, I prepared to visit my baby in the other hospital. That had been the driving force to keep me going.

I'll never forget that first special visit with Matthew. My anxious hands held him eagerly and carefully as he was connected to all sorts of devices in the incubator. Warm copious tears ran down my cheeks, but my heart was soaring as now I could hold my little one.

Quickly he became dear to us and known to us as the "little fighter." We watched him valiantly struggle for his life each day.

One day, soon after I came home with no baby, I was resting in the back room. I overheard my parents and Ron whispering in the kitchen. Thinking it was about our Matthew, I got up and asked them what was up. They looked at me glumly and stated that Ron had just checked the mail. He had received his draft notice to go to Vietnam!

My mind went spinning out of control as I wondered how I would deal with this double "cross" in my life. "Why Lord?" I asked. "Why am I the mother of a handicapped child, just like Melmark's children? Haven't I been willing to give up Martha, then Melissa? Haven't I paid my dues already in this area of babies? And now, Lord, how can I hold up Ron and entrust him solely to You in this uncertain time of war? How can I do this too?" I had much to ponder.

One night after a discouraging report from the hospital on Matthew's day, I was very restless and agitated within. I got up from the dinner table and left the house in a slow run down the street to the edge of the lake near where we lived. No one followed me as I think they knew I needed to be alone.

I was at the bottom mentally, as Matthew continued to have one bad day after another. And now he was having trouble breathing. The nurses kept telling me "not to worry," but I knew in my mother's heart he might not come home for a long time or not at all.

I sat by the lakeside and just looked at the sparkling water. God clearly brought to mind the story of Jesus walking with Peter on the seashore. The Lord asked Peter three times, "Peter, do you love Me?" Each time, Peter said, "Oh, yes, Lord." I asked myself why I was thinking of this story.

It dawned on me that possibly the Lord was asking me first of all to accept and trust Him with the fact I had a handicapped child—not a happy, healthy child with a bright future. "Yes, Lord, I love You, in spite of this."

Second, maybe I had to learn to love and trust Him to learn how to care for Matthew when he finally did come home. "Yes, even so, Lord, I love and trust You."

Third, could it be God wanted me to love and trust Him even if He decided it was best to take Matthew home to heaven? "Yes, Lord, as I cling to the broken branches of my life right now and approach this huge waterfall known as death, I confess my love for You anew. I trust You!"

Instantly, I felt a peace that I know came from Him. I knew why that story came to my mind. Another lesson. Another reminder to trust and love.

During those long eight weeks, there were countless prayer times on our knees after scary phone calls from the hospital.

I remember one such night when Matthew was about seven and a half weeks old. We called everyone we knew in our church and asked for a season of prayer for Matthew, as now he was aspirating his milk into his lungs resulting in severe weight loss and congestion in his lungs.

We literally cried out to the Lord over and over again to heal him. But as the night went on, it became clear to us that we needed to stop begging the Lord to heal him

41

and instead ask Him to do His will . . . whatever that would be. It was just like a lightbulb that went on. That was it! As much as we wanted to have Matthew as our son, alive, we needed to focus on God's will for him. When we started to pray that way, suddenly we had God's peace and were able to rest even though things looked so grim.

And so it was, in August at eight weeks old, our "little fighter" lost his battle to live and quietly slipped away from us to join his Heavenly Father. Completely healed. Able to run with two healthy legs in heaven. Safe in his heavenly Father's arms. Eight weeks of hope and heartaches came to an abrupt end. Ron and I held fast to each other in faith knowing that God does not err.

The morning before we left for the funeral, we turned on the stereo and played the Wheaton Bible

Men's choir singing "All Praise to God." That may not seem to make any sense, but we were praising the Lord with tears coming down our faces. We turned the volume way up to maximize the words so they would buoy us up for the task ahead. We were experiencing the delights of what Catherine Marshall calls "His Participating Presence."

We gathered around his tiny white casket in the graveyard, as the rain poured down. It was almost as if heaven was sharing our deep-felt grief. Broken hearts. Sad goodbyes. One last touch of the tiny casket before we turned away.

Even though the fig trees have no blossoms, and there are no grapes on the vines; even though the olive crop fails, and the fields lie empty and barren; even though the flocks die in the fields, and the cattle barns are empty, yet I will rejoice in the LORD! I will be joyful in the God of my salvation! The Sovereign LORD is my strength! He makes me as surefooted as a deer, able to tread upon the heights.

Habakkuk 3:17-19 NLT

And then one day, soon after his burial, I turned on some more inspiring hymns and began to pack away, piece by piece, another nursery. But this time, I was all alone, and it was my own child's nursery, not my sister's. I

43

reminded myself over and over, "God does not err! There was some reason for Matthew's short life. I will praise You. I must trust."

Someone has said God never wastes our pain. Our hardest tests involve our dearest loves. I can testify that God gives you the strength for hard duties when you need it—not before, not after, but just when you need it.

Lord, I see now what You mean about everything that happens being part of the lesson material in Your schoolroom. I really can praise You that You refuse to let us stay children, that you keep insisting on our growing up. Thank You for caring that much about us.[3]

This real-life experience builds a tapestry of sorts that takes on proportion, purpose, and beauty as you stand back and look at the whole sensitive piece. Beauty comes from real hurts and disappointments as well as the exciting challenges and successes. In this "loom of life" a gentle nail-pierced hand helps to weave the threads of each event through the ins and outs of life, holding the piece strongly together. This same hand holds you on your journey in the real world of our daily walk with Him.

[3] Ibid., 43.

4 ~ A Grand Plan

"For I know the plans that I have for you,"
declares the Lord,
"plans for welfare and not for calamity
to give you a future and a hope."
Jeremiah 29:11 NASB

I heard someone say once how God has a Master Plan for each one of us, all sketched out in a "map-of-sorts" in heaven. On this map, we don't know all the starts, stops, and finishes or the reasons for "pauses" along the way, as we can't see the map. The Master Creator designed this map for us to be balanced and productive for His glory. A divine Master Plan for our journey here on earth; a map for each individual. Our role is to lean on the

Everlasting Arms for the perfect heavenly outcome for each of life's happenings.

Of course, that map concept is not actually found, word for word, in the Bible, but the concept nonetheless is true. I can testify to it, especially during this next phase of my life. Here is a rendering of how His hand gently guided us along the way during this time.

After Matthew's "home-going," Ron and I prepared for his enlistment into the Armed Forces as the six month deferment they gave him for hardship flew by. And then, one snowy morning his father took him to the Army Induction Center. I watched him walk away with all that he needed in one small satchel. Twenty-some years old, married for over five years, and entering a whole new world that was challenging, physically and mentally.

He often says that one night he was sleeping in his bed with his wife, and the next night he was sleeping in a barracks with eighteen and nineteen-year-old gang members and right outside the only broken-down latrine. (Interestingly enough, Ron's group was the last division to live in these "sumptuous digs" before the building was condemned as "unlivable.")

Eight weeks later and twenty-five pounds thinner, Ron finished his basic training and signed up for Officer's Candidate School in Columbus, Georgia. This time I would be able to live nearby off base and perhaps see him on weekends if he wasn't put "on duty" for some small infraction.

The time flew by. Soon I was pinning a gold bar on his uniform and Ron was commissioned as a 2nd Lieutenant. I was so very proud of him. Because of his background in physics and success in OCS, the Army wanted him to work with an ordinance team on developing a new laser weapon system instead of going on a tour in Vietnam. As you can well imagine, I was so, so thankful to the Lord for Ron's new assignment. I still was very tender from losing Matthew and wanted to hold on tight to my husband. No Vietnam. *Thank You, Lord!*

So, off we went to our first place of duty—Huntsville, Alabama. Now to be very truthful, I must say I cried when I heard we were going there! *What's in Huntsville?* I wondered. *It's so far from home and so very hot and humid.* But being thankful it wasn't Vietnam, we packed up reluctantly and made the trip northwest to this little town. Foolishly, I didn't remember that grand plan of things in my heart of hearts. I still believed I knew best. This just didn't make sense to me.

Army officers are given houses on base with all the needed furniture and household items. This was amazing to me, and we settled in quickly. We had everything we really needed—each other, a sofa, and appropriate furniture for a three-room duplex. Everything except one small thing—an air conditioner! How can one live in 100% humidity? Somehow, we did it, as we lived on under $200 dollars a week—not enough for an air conditioner—but we were together again and happy.

Soon after getting settled, we tried going to a little church right outside of the post called Hillsboro Baptist Church. Now, when you live down South and you come from the North, you might get some "joshing" from deep down Southern members of this fellowship. They enjoyed teasing us and laughing at our northern accents, but they soon became our friends.

Southern hospitality was especially warm, and they wouldn't allow us to be Sunday-only-churchgoers. We were invited to everything, and that's just what we needed.

Soon the church approached us to be youth leaders. We were in our mid-twenties and had no attachments, so we said yes. Life became busy with church retreats, high school Bible studies, Sunday school lessons, and many other church functions.

At the same time, I found a new ob-gyn doctor in town as we still wanted children. He was younger than my doctor in New York, and he was a fertility specialist to boot. He didn't just send me home and say, "Keep trying; there is nothing wrong with you." He also put me on many fertility meds and had me go through many painful medical tests. If anyone has walked down this path, you know some of the fertility drugs produce orange size cysts on your ovaries that are very painful.

Many times, I wanted to quit and give up, but once again the Lord gently prodded me to pick up Catherine Marshall's book, *Beyond Our Selves,* and reread the chapter, "The Power of Helplessness."

> *Sometimes life finds us powerless before facts that cannot be changed.*[4] *Crisis brings us face to face with our inadequacy and our inadequacy in turn leads us to the inexhaustible sufficiency of God. This is the power of helplessness.*[5]

Those words were like a hospice to me. I asked God to use my helplessness to draw me closer to Him, to unshackle me from any thoughts of unbelief, and to remind me that ALL resources are His to use as HE sees fit.

Then, It wasn't too long when the doctor explained why pregnancy would be so very difficult for us. The diagnosis was Poly-cystic Ovaries. But that piece of news didn't seem to rattle my Southern doctor. He said he knew of one medical procedure that worked 80% of the time to help you conceive. It would be an operation called a Wedge Resection. Well, of course, we scheduled this major surgery as soon as we could.

---

[4] Catherine Marshall, *Beyond Ourselves* (New York: McGraw Hill, 1961), 146.

[5] Ibid., 150.

Now all the parts of God's Grand Plan started to come together.

As I was recuperating in the hospital, the pastor of our church, Pastor Thomas Walker, a joyful young man with a winning smile, found out that I had surgery and dropped in for a hospital visit. He expressed his concern for my health, and I assured him the reason I was there was only a "woman-plumbing" problem. I tried to keep the moment light. He didn't laugh right away but a concerned look filled his face.

I opened up and shared with him about my condition. Sadly, I recalled, "We have tried almost every fertility procedure out there to become a mom and dad . . . all to no avail! Before Ron was drafted, we even thought about a New York adoption since that was our legal residence, but the waiting list was five years. That would push us past the age limit to adopt in that state. You see there is not much hope."

He smiled and said something I will never, ever forget. "Why didn't you and Ron tell us about your problem? Don't you know the Southern Baptist church has a home for unwed Southern Baptist mothers in New Orleans? I could write you a letter of recommendation today and send it right off to them. I know of their ministry well. I love you guys so much. I'd be happy to do this for you."

I can't begin to tell you how my heart flew and fluttered within. A new bud of hope blossomed right then and there. *Oh God, is this why Ron was drafted and sent to Huntsville, Alabama? Is this why we were drawn to this church?*

And sure enough, the home studies, interviews, applications, and letters of recommendation came. This Christian adoption organization wanted to match up biological families to adoptive parents as closely as possible. They were interested in every little detail of all our family members, from number to height and personality, to help find the closest connection as possible.

Ten long months went by, and one day we got the phone call to not go away on a trip or anywhere too far without letting them know first. Wide-eyed with wonder, we speculated if the call meant it wouldn't be too many more months of waiting. Guesses . . . only guesses at that point.

Then two days later, the phone rang. We held onto the receiver like it was gold when we heard it was the agency calling again. Good news! It seems there was a baby boy about eight weeks old who they felt was just a perfect match for us. We listened in stunned silence as they explained everything about him—his raspy coo, healthy physic and nature, his big winning smile . . . We could hardly wait to see for ourselves. We were going to have a baby boy!

Several days later we gathered our baby gear in the car, including Eeyore, the blue donkey Winnie the Pooh squeeze-toy, and headed due south for a long trip to Louisiana. Each mile we traveled, the awesomeness of it began to sink in along with a sense of pure happiness. Unbelief was part of these feelings too. We just couldn't believe we were going to be parents.

I remember the trip as taking forever, but we managed to find the Southern Baptist home. We were maxed out with excitement and expectation. After we were greeted, we were ushered into a small room to sign some papers. Soon after this, they announced that they would go get our little baby. JUST LIKE THAT!

We sat there a few minutes in utter silence, listening for any sound that would bring him closer. And then we heard the happy raspy coo coming down the hallway. We edged forward in our chairs.

The staff person entered the room with this very wonderful eight-week bundle of joy. He took one look at us and a smile spread widely from ear to ear. We began to coo and make over him.

They handed him right to me. I melted and smiled as he proceeded to throw up all over the front of my dress. Even that was a joyous welcome for me as his new mother. (Years later, Brian loved that part of the story as he loves playing tricks on me to this day.)

We named our handsome baby Brian Thomas Hodge after Thomas Walker, the same man who welcomed us into his flock and then wrote us such a special letter of recommendation. We were a mom and dad now by the miracle of adoption.

The first couple of nights with Brian, I roused myself several times just to go to his room and stand there to check him and watch him sleep. I was so in love right from the start and still couldn't quite take it all in.

So, Lord, this is why You chose to bless us with a draft notice in the middle of a war, when our hearts were breaking about Matthew. This is why You had us go to that specific church! You are so powerful to turn all of the past happenings into good, guiding us each step of the way! Thank You from the bottom of our hearts for making all these moves on the Grand Map and working it out for Your glory. Thank You for blessing us in such a special way.

The story wouldn't be complete without sharing another obvious reason Ron was drafted. Remember that surgery that sent me to the hospital in the early 1970s? Well, I was one of the 80% success stories. It seemed like the surgery worked! Matthew was born in 1971. We adopted Brian in 1974, and finally in 1977 Steve was born . . . six years after the surgery.

We never knew whether the baby would be healthy or not. Our odds were 1 in 10 or 1 in a 1,000. No genetic doctor could agree. Thankfully, Ron's faith never wavered during those long nine months. I'd ask him, "What if this baby is another child with spina bifida?"

Ron, steadfast and firm, would faithfully proclaim, "There are no statistics with God. He will give us the strength to bear whatever, just at the right time, just when we need it. Have faith."

So, over and over again I set my mind on that thought. "There are no statistics with God. God will give us the strength." Just a simple "setting of the mind." Of course, some days were harder than others.

When this delivery began, husbands were allowed in the birthing room. That was such a blessing to me, as I would not be alone if there was a problem. I was wheeled into the operating room.

Ron, my overactive engineer, was just "like Ron" and into everything that was going on during delivery. He and the doctor talked like two clucking hens as Ron asked about how this and that worked and how the doctor felt about the delivery. On and on he went. That kept my mind focused and helped me not fret. And just at the right time, our sweet Stephen Paul entered the world, healthy and robust. The joy was indescribable!

Is this why I had major surgery and all those painful tests? Thank You, God. I see that now. Another part of Your miraculous master plan.

My mother sent us a letter right after Stephen's birth, as she was out of country at the time. Only my mom could put our feelings in words so beautifully.

Welcome to our world, new little one! You do not yet realize the environment of love which surrounds you on your mother's tummy, wide-eyed and content with the arms which so gratefully cuddle you, ever so gently, ever so close. How will you know how unceasingly you were prayed for, how anxiously your birth was awaited, how gratefully your life was received. ~ Nana Krentel

And then happily, three years later, I once again was pregnant. When I was in early labor for this pregnancy, we were all sitting around the kitchen table having tea as the labor began slowly. Brian was giving his Dad a back rub. (Get this, I'm in labor and Ron gets the attention!) Steve was off playing somewhere oblivious to what was happening.

Brian, who was six now and very inquisitive, looked at me from across the table and said, "Mom, did you have those kind of pains when . . ." Then he smacked his face and smiled.

My heart swelled up with love for him, and I told him to come over to me and tell me what his question was. I put my arms around him, and he said, "Oh,

Mommy, I wanted to know if you had that kind of pain when you had me. I forgot that I wasn't in your tummy."

God sent me an answer instantly. "You know, Brian, I had a different kind of pain before I got you. It was centered around my heart in the middle of my chest, and it was a pain that didn't go away. I would get it every time I saw a mother with her child at the store, or a mother pushing a stroller, and even at church when a mother would enter with an adorable child. And you know what, Brian? That pain never went away until they placed YOU in our arms."

His big infectious smile spread from one ear to another. We hugged. So, you see, in our house, when the kids ever asked about how you can get babies, we answered that there were two ways this could happen.

Anyway, that very night our precious Benjamin David arrived healthy and beautiful at 8 pounds 10 oz! Thankfully, Ron was with me again. We cried and thanked the Lord together for another perfect gift. Ron just sighed and looked at me and said, "Ahhhh . . . my three sons!"

Ronny being drafted during Vietnam? Stationed in Huntsville, Alabama? At first it seemed like the end of the world to me, but it turned out to be the beginning of the happiest time of my life. A new church and pastor, making it possible for our first adopted son. A new doctor, new diagnosis, and major surgery resulting in the birth of two more sons down the road three years apart. My ways were not His ways, but they were all part of our Master's plan.

So, you see, God is the Master Designer. Only He knows what the map says and where it is going. We just need to wait and trust Him. He has a perfect plan. We might have to wait until heaven to see the reason for some of life's happenings, but sometimes He allows us to see clearly what He had in mind while we are here on earth. Our job, in the meantime, is to keep looking up and trusting our great God as we go along. We should remember this and have more faith as we face some of the hurtles on the journey. They are all charted out on a map-of-sorts in heaven with our names on it.

5 ~ A Mother's Journal

*"Home is a lot of things . . . but mainly
it is the place where life makes up its mind."*
Charles R. Swindoll

Raising our three boys was chock-full of hugs and kisses, love, skinned knees, black eyes, quibbles, laughs, fears, and a "Hodge-Podge" of pandemonium! I loved every moment of those days, but I also felt a great responsibility to do it all "right" . . . how I dreamt it should be done. Some days I was just plain worn out trying.

Being one who would always analyze my Christian progress, along the way I often found myself becoming overwhelmed and feeling like the job was too great. So, to the Lord I would have to run to confess my inadequacies to do the job alone. He would gently agree with me and remind me, "Yes, it is too big for you alone. Lean on Me; I will help you!"

The LORD will perfect that which concerneth me . . .
forsake not the works of thine own hands.
Psalm 138:8 KJV

Being a parent and navigating through the times of nurturing babies, chasing toddlers, and watching three individuals grow and exert themselves, I learned many valuable lessons that added to my patience and perseverance. I watched as my boys tried to move away from total dependency. Yet, I still saw they needed us more than ever.

I questioned in my journal, *Can I let them go? Not embarrass them when they think for themselves? Let them experience some decisions on their own? Can I let them develop skills by maybe having failures? Can I give them up to let them play a little more freely? Farther away?* TRUST was at the bottom of most of those questions.

And the "Matthew-factor" played a part in my nervousness and ability to trust more. As a result, I was a "mother hen" clucking over each situation the boys experienced . . . over-careful . . . over-holding on tight at times. I humbly admit I was often called the "worrywart."

Here are a few journal entries written during this time of being a mom of three wonderful wiggly boys. Somehow, I found time to write things down back then. I wonder how I did that? Some will make you smile, some you can probably relate to, and some are reminders to me today as a parent of grown children.

Steve at two, beginning to express himself better word-wise. Oh, such an active boy—exhausting me with his climbing and ability to be a "little dickens" in all situations. When eating, food is all over him and everywhere else. When shopping, Steve somehow wiggles out of the stroller. And in the middle of the night, Steve makes "tiger-screams" to get our attention. He loves to pull a chair all over the house to climb into and on things precariously. Besides these cute things, he is most of all, a real love. *Loves the hugs and kisses! Is a Pop-Pop fan through and through!*

Ben at four . . . When we were praying at night, Ben said he wanted to ask Jesus to come in his heart. He was concerned that the Devil could get in if he didn't do it right away. (This was about the time *Star Wars* was such a rage.) Then he asked, "Is Jesus kind of like a 'force-field' in your heart?" This concept obviously made him feel safe. *What a great symbolic picture! He was always thinking!*

I need to learn, over and over again, not to expect spiritual maturity from babes. Here is a perfect example. One night Pastor came over to instruct Brian before he was to be baptized at church. Right in the middle of this long discourse, Brian interrupted politely and said, "Pastor, I hate to change the subject, but I wonder if you would tell me something I have wondered about for a long time now?"

I was elated as I watched Brian. He seemed so sincere and genuinely interested!

Brian continued, "Did the stone kill Goliath or did he die when David cut off his head?" *Cringe. But I couldn't help but smile inside as I've wondered that myself.*

Another time: When I asked Brian what he wanted to be when he grew up, Brian answered thoughtfully, "Just myself, Mom." *Priceless!*

Benji has been especially a joy to us recently. His love for the Lord is remarkable. There was a special drawing he made on Easter Sunday. It read quite simply, "TO JESUS, I LOVE YOU—BENJI."

He was very insistent that he wanted this note to go to Jesus. I suggested we put it in the offering plate.

He said, "No, when I die, tape it here on my chest. Jesus will see it when I go up there."

Oh, what simple, yet profound faith!

My new trial is a lack of quiet time. There is an interruption every five minutes it seems. I don't want to resent those interruptions, but this week I have been so short with the children. I can remember the other day, after devotions, I knelt down for a quick prayer. The boys saw me there on my knees and jumped on my back thinking I was going to be their "pony-boy!" *My prayer is to have a servant's heart in times like these and that I will learn to pray "on the go."*

Today, Stevie put up a "hissy fit" when I asked him to come in. It was such a big one that I thought the behavior deserved a spanking when Daddy came home. Up in his room, all on his own Steve wrote sentences, a thank you letter, and drew me a picture. He even washed his own mouth out with soap! When Dad appeared, he announced he was ready for him. He was sitting on the bed waiting. We found out later he had put on three pairs of pants under his heavy sleeper to better prepare for his spanking. *What a dickens!*

Brian's room looks like a tornado hit after he's been cleaning for an hour. Steve pushed Benji down the stairs. Ben just threw up all over the rug. I just lost a check. After much "trying otherwise," I lost my cool totally. Somedays,

I reason I have every logical or worldly right to throw a real "fit" myself in the middle of everything.

But I'm finding at the heart of *every* problem, lies the HEART. My heart has tendencies to be reminded over and over again that I need to be grafted into God in order for the fruit of the Spirit to be seen, in spite of life's circumstances, in the crucible of our home. How shall I lead my children unless I have the fruit I yell at them to have.

I need to chisel away at my heart and ask the Lord to help me again so I can walk worthy of Him and bring into captivity every thought to obedience in Christ. Righteous words come from a righteous heart—one surrendered to Him, cleansed by Him, and filled with thoughts He strives to place there.

I need to always remember that my children reflect perfectly all my faults. *I have to be aware that my life either sheds light or casts a shadow!*

Steve is the picture of Dennis the Menace. So cute and yet such a "little rascal" getting himself knee-deep in trouble all the time! His heart, however, is always so attuned to the Spirit, and he often gets teary when speaking of the Lord. His piano is coming well, but I must push him every day to sit down and practice. He wiggles and flies all over the bench, and yet somehow music comes out. He has a beautiful touch. He just can't get enough hugs and kisses!

Benji at five years old is our constant chatterbox. Today he announced again about how he was born.

"Mom, I know where I came out!"

"You do?" I said.

"Yes, from a little secret door!" he exclaimed. "But how did I get out of the little secret door?"

I just listened.

"I know," he continued. "Jesus was in your heart and He pushed me out." Then he said, "You weren't too happy when you saw me!"

"No?" I said. "Why?"

"Well, Mommy, in the picture you looked kind of bad!"

We had a nice follow up talk. *So creative!*

Brian returned from camp all in one piece but with a black eye. He said it came from swimming into an inner tube nozzle! He had a wonderful time, and I'm so glad. It seemed he survived even when I wasn't there to nag.

My prayer for him all week was that he might desire to begin his walk alone with God in the way of having his own devotions.

Last night while we were in the kitchen, he said to me, "I can't believe it, Mom, but some kids are really psyched out about reading the Bible." He went on to say that made a real impression on him and that he knows he should read the Bible too. *Oh, I pray for that first step and thank our Father for the desire.*

Well, Benji is in school now. The night before he was really heavy about the whole thing. He started to cry and told me he didn't want to leave me. Oh me! I hugged and hugged him to no avail. Then I said, "How would you like mom to buy a little Matchbox car for you if you are good and have it waiting for you by lunchtime?"

Well, the frown disappeared and he said, "How about a little transformer?" Well, he's not dumb.

Then we also talked about pinning on a little calico brave heart on his shirt. Then every time he missed me, he could cover the little heart with his hand and he would feel brave. He liked that idea and was sure to remind me of it the next morning. So, I cut out a calico red heart and asked him where I should pin it—on top or under his shirt. Well, it had to be right out on top so he could see it!

When he came home, he said, "Boy, that calico heart really helped me!" He had a super day and left me with a smile! Praise the Lord the two older boys seem to be very enthusiastic about their day and their teachers too. What an answer to prayer this was.

The other night around the table we were discussing a family who is brokenhearted over a son who has rejected Christ and is involved in some sort of trouble all the time.

Well, Stevie was caught up in the whole story. He spurted out, "I know what I'd do. I'd take him right up to his room and give him a spanking until he asked Jesus into his heart."

We all broke up with laughter!

For the last few days the house has been full of endless chatter, little footsteps running around, adults laughing, and kid's squabbling.

We've had company from our old church, back-to-back. The visits were such rewarding times of fellowship. It just amazes me how, in the body of Christ, we can live so closely with one another and feel comfortable even when we haven't seen each other for years.

Of course, there were times during the visiting when I wanted to crawl under the tablecloth like when Stevie came out in the middle of dinner one night with just one simple word . . . the word "D. . . ."

We asked with red faces, "What did you say?" Assuredly he said again, "D . . . !" even louder.

We said, "Do you know that is a bad word?" He innocently said he didn't even know what "D" meant.

Oh well, those friends got an earful. We were humbled.
What the bus ride and school teaches your child! Our
Dennis the Menace!

Benji was pestering me relentlessly when I had a
neighbor over for coffee. I turned to him in jest and said,
"Benji, I'm going to change my name to George, so I don't
hear Mommy, Mommy, heh, Mommy."

He said nothing and just grinned. Well, my friend and
I went on chatting together for some time before Benji got
up to get his coat to go outside. As he walked away down
the hall, he peeked around the corner and said, "Oh, bye,
George, I'll be outside!" *Laughter!*

Each day I gather the boys in my arms before they
leave for school. I pretty much pray the same prayer each
day. I ask the Lord to help them be "little Daniels" in
school and to grow to love Him with all their heart.

I love them so deeply, and I remind myself that God
is not only just concerned for them, like I am, but He
loves my "little men" even MORE than I do! I just need
to open up my firm grip on them, like in the Prayer of
Relinquishment. When I am able to let go, parenting
becomes more of God's business and not fully mine
anymore. My load becomes so much lighter when I remind
myself of this important truth.

Christmas is fast approaching. The kitchen stove is constantly "on" it seems. The fireplace is a warm glow, and the kids are all hyper. In all the excitement and festivity, we're finding it hard to concentrate on the true meaning of Christmas. So, we decided to invite all the neighborhood children over for a Christmas party where I would tell the real Christmas story. The invitations all clearly stated that was the purpose and asked them to dress up like a character at the nativity scene. It also said we would end the night by going out caroling.

Fifteen children showed up and sat there on the floor with wide eyes during the flannelgraph story of the nativity. Suddenly, I stopped and asked them to raise their hands if this was the first time they heard this story. Many raised their hands. Then I quickly added, "How many would like to hear more about this Jesus?"

Hands waved above their tiny heads. God is good! (This was the beginning of a Bible Club in our neighborhood every Thursday after school for several years. God really blessed our group. Some wonderful times spent in the Bible!)

And now the journal sits in the book cabinet to be pulled out, shared, and laughed over on family occasions, but mostly to remind us that God has a plan for each one of my boys.

Now they are raising children of their own. In their journey of child-rearing I would love them to remember:

> *Listen . . . you must love the LORD your God with all your heart, all your soul, and all your strength. And you must commit yourselves wholeheartedly to these commands that I am giving you today. Repeat them again and again to your children. Talk about them when you are at home and when you are on the road, when you are going to bed and when you are getting up* (Deuteronomy 6:4-7 NLT).

6 ~ What's in Your Sandbox?

"How do you spell 'love?'" – Piglet
"You don't spell it, you feel it." Pooh

You've probably heard the saying, "Play in your own sandbox." Children always like to play in a sandbox where hours can be spent in imaginary make-believe. Every sandbox seems to have rules that must be followed so that the sandbox environment is safe and fun. *No throwing the sand, as it could get in someone's eyes. Don't break down someone else's sandcastle because that's not kind and somebody will cry . . .*

The environment of a sandbox must be a place where children feel safe to explore and imagine as they play with the children who join them. Everything runs smoothly when the rules are followed.

Just like having the perfect sandbox, a child's home environment must be carefully honed into a safe, happy, and secure place for them to grow.

Now I guess being a teacher for over fifteen years, makes me a little bossy and strong-willed about child-rearing. As I raised my boys and taught many children, I aimed to make the following ideas work. Some were a success; others were real failures. However, when missing the mark, I always climbed back up on this podium and tried again. Please bear with this "old" teacher and mom as she shares some insights from past successes and failures.

So, the question is: What kind of home setting gives a child a sense of stability and well-being?

• **Loving?** Do we practice displays of affection—hugs, kisses, pats of approval? Do we make opportunities for verbalizing our love to the child no matter what the circumstances are?

Every day we should look for creative ways to compliment our child for some sought behavior or special trait. Stickers, ribbons, star charts, and verbal praise go a long way to creating a loving environment.

Do we model what love looks like in the ho-hum of life?

Do we show love to our mate in front of our child or grandchild? Children derive a sense of security when they know mom and dad are happy together.

Do we try to avoid conflict in front of the family? When conflict is unavoidable, do we model effective ways to resolve conflicts. Do we let our child hear us say, "I'm sorry"?

• **Happy?** Do we work on being enthusiastic about things? Children can sense when we'd rather be elsewhere but with them. Are we happy deep down as we live out our lives? Do we model positive behaviors such as whistling while we work or singing a happy tune?

Children are like thirsty sponges who take in every vibe we send out—all the unspoken ones, as well as the overt ones. They read us like a book! What messages are they picking up from our behavior in our home?

• **Structured, yet spontaneous?** Most children thrive in a structured environment where they know how things work, who is in charge, what the schedule is for the week, etc. This structure should not be so rigid that spontaneity is squelched.

Reflecting a delight in discovering new things or doing something "outside of the box" is catching as well. But structure is the foundation for security. A child learns what to expect and has a sense of security. *Mommy usually reads me two stories and sings two songs before I take my nap.*

Each year, when teaching my 1st grade students, it was always a very manageable task because of a routine and structure that we established the first six weeks of school. The structured classroom environment promoted security and safety as the children knew what to do and what was expected. The first six weeks were like "boot-camp."

We practiced for fun, lining up in proper order for the bus ride home, how to check-in in the morning and sign out in the afternoon, how to walk in the hallway, and other daily routines. Before long, the kids knew basic self-care routines to make school life easier.

This classroom management created a sense of well-being and security so needed for children in school. Soon the children were even able to internalize these newly acquired routines and apply them to other similar routines. Happy children were the outcome of such practices.

All children need routines to provide a strong foundation in their lives and to grow in confidence and self-discipline. Knowing what is expected allows them to feel secure and to understand how they can be successful.

• **Creating "Me Time" and "Me Space"?** Parenting is one of the hardest jobs out there. Sometimes we feel the need to recharge with time by ourselves. Children feel that need as well. Everyone needs space some time throughout the day.

It's important to provide this space for your child. A child's own room can be his "Me Space." If your child does not have a room of his own, create a place that is his own space to read, to play, to think, and to keep his own things. Creatively, the space could be a tent, a blanket fort, a space under the stairs, under a bed with a flashlight, an oversized closet or box, or a tree fort etc. The skies the limit!

Sometimes life is so stimulating for a child that they need to be quiet for an hour or so. That means sending home who else is in the sandbox so regrouping and recharging can occur.

• **Exposing a child to opportunities for spiritual growth?** Today the number of children going to Sunday

School classes or youth groups at church is only a small majority of children. By the time children are in high school, 75% will drop out of church activities. We only have a small window to help cultivate a deep understanding about God and a relationship with Him. Whether it is a Bible club, youth group, or Christian camp, the priority to make this happen is utmost!

One of my most lasting impressions of my father was coming down the stairs each morning and seeing him in a full-dress suit kneeling to pray in his quiet time. What message do you think that sent to me? Priceless. What do our children see of our walk with the Lord?

• **Promoting strong family ties?** Do we gather at least once a day in a place where the whole family can be together to share with one another? The dinner hour is a time when families can learn from each other and develop unity as a group.

Do we placate our children too much with television and movies just for some peace and quiet? Are we too involved in our technical toys to show interest in communicating with them?

Reading, playing, walking, and talking promotes strong family ties. "Talk as you walk" is not only great for increasing a child's word comprehension and building on prior knowledge, it also builds strong relationships with one another.

Do we establish yearly routines for family fun? Do we take a vacation together, building meaningful memories? Are there holiday visits to relatives? Is our child developing a strong bond with others in his extended family? Writing letters, sleepovers, and sharing birthday celebrations builds a sense of belonging and a sense of family.

Do we commemorate the family in scrapbooks, slideshows etc. to mark special occasions?

- **Listening? Talking *with* and not *at* a child throughout the day?** When our children talk to us, do we have good eye contact to show we are truly listening? Do we stop everything to listen? Do we stoop down and get on their eye level? If a child thinks we aren't listening to the small things they have to tell us, they won't share the bigger things that may be on their minds. Be an eager listener!

- **Exercising praise for positive behaviors we observe?** *I just love the way you help Mommy pick up the toys. You are such a responsible boy!* A few positive words or pats on the back go a long way in making someone feel proud of himself and able to "reach the sky." Praise, praise, and more praise . . . There can't ever be too much! But it needs to be commensurate to a real positive behavior. No counterfeits! Kids know!

- **Following through consistently when boundaries are over-stepped?** *Mommy told you that if you continued to hit Billy, you would have to sit in the No-No* *chair.* Then make sure, on the first reminder, that the consequence is carried out! Not after the second or third infraction. Kids learn really fast who means what they say and who doesn't.

Be firm but controlled. Letting a situation escalate to the anger level means that boundaries and follow-through haven't been clearly delineated in the past and the child knows that.

• **Modeling positive behaviors for children to imitate?** *Watch Joey say "please" when he wants another cookie. Isn't that polite and good? I know you can do that too!* If children see you modeling and praising the behavior you are trying to teach them, the impression it makes is imprinted in their minds. Children always look up to you to firmly lead the way.

Another way this might work is rewarding targeted behaviors with positive rewards. Let's say you have had some difficulty with "Johnny" being polite in public . . . You set up a token system which is not only fun but practically makes the child focus in on the desired result. *Every time I see you say please and thank you, a token goes in the Happy Jar.* This builds up to some desired end—ice cream or a token toy. I have used this successfully from everything from potty-training to limiting "hissy-fits" for attention when things go wrong.

• **Responding appropriately to upsetting situations?** The more you coddle a child with too much sympathy when something little happens to upset him, the more you lose an opportunity to teach the child resiliency.

Resiliency will be needed all through his life. A way to develop this key trait is to model problem-solving or working through a problem calmly with clear steps and words. Showing the child that the circumstance is not past helping, and they will make it through the problem using key helps, would be the best option. During times like these we need to lighten up on the sympathy and brainstorm together positive suggested ways to rectify the situation.

• **Sharing honestly and calmly with a child why you are displeased when an infraction occurs?** At the same time, we need to let them know they are loved and valued in spite of what happened. Balance is important here. It's also important to do this as close in time as possible to the infraction. If you wait too long, the child has already moved on to new things that demand his attention.

• **Building behaviors to produce intrinsic motivation for future patterns of behavior?** *Don't you feel good inside when you help others with a happy spirit?* If a child learns that he will receive a certain positive feeling inside from doing something right, the behavior will be much better reinforced. Not all disciplines and directives should be extrinsic. The child can learn better if he sees the benefits of positive behaviors in making himself happier. All on his own!

Well, these are just a few suggestions to "noodle on." This season might be a good time to take stock and make sure your home sandbox is one where children can feel safe and be nurtured at the same time as they develop character and good behavior. Take some of these ideas to heart from an old teacher and flawed mother. You only have one chance to do it right with God's help. Think about it.

7 ~ Nighttime Visitor

For the angel of the LORD is a guard;
He surrounds and defends all who fear Him.
Psalm 34:7 NLT

C rime always happens to somebody else, not you. That's usually what everyone thinks way down deep. But, of course, this is not always the case.

I remember the night so well. It was July 7th, in a little town called Jeffersonville near Phillie. Ron and I were preparing for a good night of rest. Brian, Steve, and Benji were already fast asleep.

After the lights were out and a "one more check" of the boys was completed, we fell into bed and marveled how we didn't even need the window unit air conditioner. The mainline Phillie area is known for its hot and humid weather in July. Hard to sleep weather. The window air conditioner in our bedroom was the only AC in the house. We usually closed our door to keep at least one bedroom cool. The kids knew they could bring in their sleeping bags if they couldn't sleep as they only had a fan in their rooms.

Normally, our air ran all night on high with the door closed. But tonight, there was a gentle breeze blowing through our opened windows so we never turned the air on at all. Very unusual for July.

Instead of AC, Ron turned the floor fan on, as we are used to sleeping with a gentle purrrr somewhere in the room. A few minutes later, for some reason, the fan started making this rattling noise. Ron got up and turned it off with a grumpy moan. No air conditioner or fan to lull him to sleep! Finally, we settled ourselves with just the windows open and the quiet breeze wafting in slowly. Everything was still.

Sleep came quickly after a busy day. Around three a.m. I awoke with a start. I had had a horrible, vivid dream! The nightmare made me sit straight up, wide-eyed, in bed.

To my chagrin, I dreamt Ron had some sort of disease and was dying. My adrenaline was running in full-gear now and my heart beat double-quick in realistic grief.

Rubbing my eyes in an attempt to wipe the dream away, I slowly began to come back to my senses. I reached over and kissed my sleeping husband, grateful it was only a dream. Then I pulled and poked at our comforter, arranging it carefully over us, as it was a little cool by this time. For some reason, I did not go down the hall into each of the boys' rooms to make sure they were covered. This was usually a nightly routine for me. Not tonight for some reason.

I laid there waiting for my heart to completely calm itself, when I heard the slightest creak in the floor down the hallway near the boys' rooms.

Now usually, if the kids wake up trying to find the bathroom in the middle of the night, my routine was to ask who was up to make sure they were awake enough to find the bathroom and not the stairs. So, I yawned and called out, "Okay, who's up?"

Usually, one of the boys would respond, "It's just me, Mom. I'm awake." But this time there was no response. Normally, I would have jumped up to help them find the bathroom but for some reason not tonight.

Then I heard the creak again. Quiet footsteps! Now I was beginning to get a little irritated. I called out in my teacher's voice this time. "All right, who's up?" No response. Still, for some reason I did not get up.

I thought to myself that this bad dream must have rattled me so much that I was imagining things. Then I heard a loud thump, thump, thump, THUMP" banging down each one of our stairs. Something or someone was in a big hurry. They were heavy footsteps with the sound of change rattling in a pocket.

What is Brian doing with change in his jammies? I wondered. *But . . . he has no pockets.*

Then it slowly dawned on me that the thumps were made by someone a lot heavier than Brian. Someone big. It didn't compute at first. How could someone have breached the inner sanctity of our home, coming upstairs into our bedrooms? Into my children's rooms! It took a couple of long seconds for that to sink in.

Suddenly, I went into full command-mode. I jumped over Ron's sleeping body and ran to the front window. Would my scream come out when I opened my mouth? What if this was nothing more than my imagination? I would be so embarrassed tomorrow trying to explain why I was screaming out our bedroom window to our close-knit neighborhood. But I was quite certain something was gravely amiss, and out came the largest cry for help you have ever heard!

To this day, I still can hardly believe what was sitting at the bottom of our short driveway. A police car! I could clearly see a policeman inside as his interior lights were on. He quickly jumped out of his car. The Lord knew I probably wouldn't have been able to even dial 911.

The next minute played out in slow motion in my mind, but really happened quite quickly. Ron was fully awake by now, but I was literally holding him back from going downstairs. I begged him to stay upstairs until the police officer was at the door as I surmised whoever was downstairs was quite heavy and a lot bigger than us. Ron would be in danger then.

I also began to check on the boys. Everyone was still sleeping, except Benji, as he heard me scream. I gathered him in my arms. He was fine.

Within seconds there were loud knocks on the front door. Ron made his way downstairs to let the police in. For some strange reason, all the lights were turned on when Ron got downstairs. I stayed upstairs with the boys, walking around in a weird, stunned daze. You hear of people breaking in to steal, but not so much about robbers coming upstairs. All this was running through my head as I listened to Ron and the policeman thoroughly searching downstairs and through the garage.

After about ten minutes, I heard them talking more calmly and I realized the "coast must be clear," so I came down the stairs gingerly. Presently, more policeman came in and started to look again just in case they missed something. All to no avail. I just stood there stunned with Benji in my arms. Brian and Steve still slept soundly through all the commotion.

The policemen then went outside to hunt throughout the neighborhood. They observed how the intruder had stolen two benches from our neighbor's lawn furniture and stacked them haphazardly on top of each other to crawl through our dining room window we had inadvertently left open. My purse sat there on the dining room table like a proud hen . . . untouched.

Soon the police said they had looked everywhere possible and that they were leaving the neighborhood. They would send someone over for fingerprinting soon. We were advised to just go back to sleep for it was still dark. RIGHT! My eyes were as wide as an owl's by now, and I was on-duty, full alert mode.

We climbed back in bed holding Benji. Ron put his arms around us and promptly went back to sleep! *Men!*

An hour or so later, the sun started to come up and I heard the police cars pulling into our driveway. I went downstairs to let them in. Ron, still half asleep, followed me. They announced they had captured the intruder! My heart lightened.

Come to find out, they hadn't all left the neighborhood in the middle of the night as they said. They left one policeman hiding in the bushes. The plan, unbeknownst to us, was to have him watch for the intruder to come back to his car parked near the woods in the cul-de-sac behind our house near the woods.

And that is just what happened. The intruder had drugs in his possession and was high when he was caught. As I listened to all the details from the officer who caught him, I busied myself scrambling up some eggs and bacon for the policemen. I was beginning to breathe normally again.

"But, Officer," I asked, "why didn't this man take my purse sitting right there on the table?"

He paused and said, "Mrs. Hodge, we didn't want to alarm you, but this intruder is not 'that kind' of burglar. His intent was to hurt someone sexually." I froze as he continued. "We have staked out this man's apartment over and over again, for years now, trying to catch him after one of his trysts. He does his dastardly deed right after he turns on all the lights on the first floor of wherever he goes. All your lights were on too. It is kind of his identifying mark. He probably was looking for a girl's bedroom when you heard him."

Then, it slowly dawned on me . . . our guardian angel was with us in a very real way this whole July evening. The Lord must have sent him by allowing me to have a bad dream, so I would be awake. There was no AC or fan rattling so I could hear. I didn't get up to cover the boys and thus didn't run into the intruder in the hallway all alone. And a police car was sitting right there at the end of our driveway so we could be rescued immediately! These were not mere coincidences; these were the hand of the Lord protecting our family.

The next day I took a walk around the block with the kids to the cul-de-sac right behind our house. A neighbor, who I hadn't met, came out of his house just to introduce himself to me. (The whole neighborhood had heard about it by noon of the next day, of course.)

"I have to tell you this," he said. "Once a night, I usually have to get up to use the facilities. Typically, I do "my business" and hurry back to bed. But last night, for some reason, I looked out the window and there was a van parked in the street. I watched as a man in a full-dress suit got out and walked behind the house across the street, straight toward your house. I thought to myself, *He has a hot date, or he is up to no good.* So, I decided to call the police. I didn't have a good feeling. I never have called the police before, but something prompted me to pick up the phone."

Another evidence of our guardian angel protecting us! Thank You, Lord.

God's protection during this night was like a miracle to me . . . so many signs of His hand being on our house. From that moment on, anyone who stopped and talked with us heard the full story from me how God miraculously worked to surround us. I would testify about all the factors that the Lord engineered to keep us from succumbing to this evil.

Yes, in this imperfect, sinful world, men like these sow their terrible deeds, ruining their victims for a lifetime.

As a result of this man being caught that evening, a new mug shot was taken. The young girls who were violated by him in the past were able to identify him clearly. Fingerprints were collected and matched, and he was sent to prison for thirteen years.

Yes, bad things happen in our lives, but God is ever present and sends us help along the way to face whatever it is we have to face.

Do we ever focus on this reality? Or do we rest on the fact that we live in a good neighborhood, or have good locks and double bolts, or a guard dog, or better yet, a home security system? Again, I can testify,

> *If you make the LORD your refuge,*
> *if you make the Most High your shelter,*
> *no evil will conquer you;*
> *no plague will come near your home.*
> *For He will order his angels*
> *to protect you wherever you go.*
> *They will hold you up with their hands*
> *so you won't even hurt your foot on a stone.*
> Psalm 91:9-12 NLT

Oh, by the way, I didn't run out and buy a huge dog or even have a security system put in, like I honestly wanted to and was considering the next day. Instead, when Ron left for his many business trips, I just focused on the facts of this night.

There are no coincidences with Him. Our *real* night-time visitor was an angel. Each occurrence that happened this night was a "God-thing!" I am convinced! We have a powerful God. I need to remember this always.

Praise be to God!

8 ~ Old Age Is Not for Sissies

*"In life, we only stay young long enough
to strengthen our backs for the burden of old age."*
Beth Moore

Have you noticed that for each new phase of life, there seems to be great preparation and celebration preceding it? It's obvious proof that you are preparing your way to enter a whole new phase. For example, the wonder of young love and marriage, planning the "perfect marriage" ceremony, attending marriage seminars, celebrating anniversaries . . .

Then, another phase begins—the excitement of getting ready for a new baby, learning how-to classes on breathing and labor, painting the nursery, studying manuals on discipline and care, buying scrapbooks and cameras . . .

Even for our mid-life there are more preparations: celebrating the joys of raising a family; attending graduations, weddings, and baby showers while entering the height of a promising career . . . The experiences build on one another to prepare us for each stage of life we are entering.

And then, the "harvest" age comes, and we find ourselves in an unfamiliar journey. Old age! It sneaks up on us when we are in the prime of life. Suddenly, we are in a new world, and we've had little to no preparation. No map, instruction manual, or encouraging seminars to navigate through its deep challenges.

Physically, our bodies are telling us mentally that the two are no longer in sync. Our children look at us with unbelief as if we can snap out of it.
Mildred Krentel

Our extended family watch us as if we have always been old and discount what we try to say and do. Yet, inside, we feel as if we still are young and wonder why they can't quite see it.

As we look around for the "normal" button for this period of life, we can learn from others going through these waters and how they navigated around certain challenges. I learned many things about old age taking care of my mother as she lived to ninety-two. She was sharp and alert right to the end. She wanted to finish up "right" she would say, but she would often leave me with lessons I needed to get "right" as I took care of her.

Here is one short entry from my own Mother's journal about having a birthday in old age:

Why is it each and every year, on one special day, we locate those short stubby sticks of paraffin hiding in a kitchen drawer and place them, one by one, in the middle of a mound of sweet stuff on top of a cake we call our "birthday cake"? Each year we sing "Happy Birthday to you." But along with each successive birthday, life seems to lose a little of that giddy happiness we felt when we blew out sweet sixteen.

Why? I think I know. As I have now amassed almost ninety of these occasions, I know for sure that "old age is not for sissies." There are many of you that know these are the years your feet hurt before they even hit the floor, your head aches, and your joints protest. You grab your raincoat only to discover your eyes have tricked you again and produced the foggy world you think you see out the window. Your eyeglasses are all smeared again, and the sun is shining gloriously. Things are not as they seem.

It occurs to me that it is high time indeed to prepare ourselves for the end of the race. We want to finish the race gloriously even though some of us belong to a motley group of gray-haired puff-a-billies limping for the goal posts. If it were left up to me, I'd like nothing better than to pull off my sneakers for good and hang my feet up, but it looks like I'll be here on earth for the full count.

Mildred Krentel

When you are a caregiver, you are learning as you go through the process of taking care of your mother or father. Here are a few things I learned from my dear mom, as I took care of her. I'm praying they will help you as you deal with your elderly loved one or as you begin to navigate through the old age stage of someone dear to you!

Don't drop in on the elderly and ask, "Hi, how are you doing?" or "How are you feeling?" I found out these are not favorite questions.

Some days Mom just wanted to forget that her legs weren't working like they used to, or her back was absolutely killing her, or she had just lost her keys, had a fender-bender, etc. Reciting a litany of aches and pains and misfortunes just sometimes makes it harder.

My Grandma Rix used to always answer these questions with a twinkle in her eye and a smile on her wrinkled face, saying, "With my fingers, dearie! Just 'a-feelin' with my fingers!"

My mother would be more interested in what was going on in our lives instead of answering questions. That provided her with a nice diversion to the pains of her aging body and "ho-hum" of living in a nursing home.

Here's another tip. Make sure to ask what your parent has been doing. Take time to listen and sit in one place for more than a few minutes as it may take a little longer some days for her to share what she wants to say.

My tendency when visiting was jumping up and fixing something or doing a much-needed chore. I always had a "to-do" list for our visit together, as there was so much to do. I was so wrong. Mom just wanted to sit and talk or do something totally off the wall. So, I really had to work on settling myself to fulfill this idea.

My mother was always writing her latest book. Many times, my urgent job became one of just being a good listener as she proudly read to me her latest and greatest. These quiet times of listening to her creative words underscored her relevance and creativity, even at her late age.

One good thing I did sometimes was clearing my schedule, packing my suitcase, and coming to visit for a couple of nights. This really delighted Mom. This made for extra time to talk late into the evening, enjoy an early morning coffee time together, and have extra time to look at the catalogues etc. It was a blessing to invest in her with extra time!

Let your elderly parent "show" you off to all her friends. Often when visiting Mom, it was important for her to introduce me to as many friends as she could during my stay. It's been my experience that it was kind of like "Show and Tell" time at school, and the object to be shown was me! I felt I was "on display" in some invisible store window that Mom made for me.

It was so important to her that I carve out some time to go to dinner with her, sit in the dining room at her table, go to a hymn sing with her, and play Scrabble with her and her friends. These "show off" times warmed her soul and were well worth the effort.

My mother moved to an independent care place near our home when I was teaching first grade. Things became challenging as Mom thought I had all the time in the world to spend with her after I finished teaching at 5 p.m. She would say, "Can't Ronny take care of himself tonight so you can stay longer?"

This was hard on me, as I used to worry I wasn't staying long enough all the time anyway! I also thought if I announced up front how long I had to stay that might help with this problem. My recommendation is, don't do that. She hated it when I would come in saying, "Hi Mom, I only have about thirty minutes before I have to get home to fix dinner, but I can't wait to hear how your day has been." Not good.

Honestly, you never can stay long enough for an elderly parent. Don't have any expectations that a certain amount of time will be adequate. That is the long, hard truth of the matter.

Older parents soar when they see their loved ones, and they don't want to go back to being lonely and down after you leave. Their loneliness is like a deep hole they can't climb out of, and sometimes you are that ladder to rescue them for a while. That's what you need to remember. It might never seem to be enough, but your visit did provide some temporary relief and comfort.

Remember that your loved one feels twenty-five years old inside and thinks everyone else at the nursing home are the "old ones." Mother used to say everyone living there were so old they just were waiting to die.

Oh my! Because we loved her, we consciously had to make her life experiences as happy as we could. Putting up and taking down her holiday decorations, taking her out shopping, including her in our family gatherings, bringing her fresh flowers, going out to eat (she loved that), taking her out shopping or to church, including her on our vacations—all these things were what her twenty-five-year-old personality would like to do. This took her mind off her surroundings and hopefully made her feel that life was worth living and that she didn't have to hang out with only those "old" people all the time.

If you have to take over and help with the finances, it is important you do that carefully. Always make sure you include your loved one in what you are doing even if you could do it more quickly without taking the time to run everything by her. A once-a-week meeting to go over her finances will make her feel more needed in the decisions and give her some ownership in her finances. That's important to an elderly parent.

Protecting her pocketbook is another tip for success in keeping your elderly mother happy. Where does one begin? Of utmost importance: Always make sure she has an "in style" pocketbook, and check that money is in her wallet each week. Even though she might not be driving or going out of the nursing home, there is still the desire to buy a milkshake or other treat or to purchase a gift for someone else. Mom always found things to buy or ways to treat others! Mom's credit cards were also important to her, and we still used them when shopping online.

The day my mom died, I was sitting by her side holding her hand. Most of the time her eyes were closed, but they suddenly popped open as she had something to say. "Diane, go get my pocketbook!"

Now I knew because Mom was sleeping so much a family member removed everything of value for safe-keeping. But I looked around and there was her empty Michael Kors purse.

She continued, "Bring it here!"

I did as I was told, and she fished around in there for her wallet. I could see all the charge cards were gone and things looked pretty empty. But suddenly her hand was waving wildly, and she said, "I want you to have this!"

Lo and behold, she found a ten-dollar bill and proudly held it up to me. Mind you, there was nothing else in the wallet. I don't know where she had tucked it.

She announced firmly, "I want you to have this."

I was touched. She was serious. I thanked her but reminded her I couldn't take her last ten-dollar bill. "Why,

Mom," I told her, "you could buy some ice cream with it. Hold on to it!" I encouraged.

She begrudgingly put it away as she was too tired to argue with me. That was just like her, always looking to make someone else's day and to unselfishly make life as exciting as she could.

By the way, after she passed away, I made sure someone got me her purse out of her room. I retrieved the ten-dollar bill to pin on my bulletin board at home as a memory of her generosity.

So, don't forget having money in their own wallet is important to your loved one even when living in a nursing home and being in their nineties. For that reason, each week when I was POA, I made sure she carried $200 in cash for anything she wanted to spend it on. She always felt empowered!

If I had the chance, I would love another talk with my mom and would ask forgiveness for all the times I rushed her, didn't really have time to listen, and other oversights I made. She deserved much better, but there were no manuals and instructions for this time of life—just what we learned the hard way.

Old age is a rugged pathway to our eternal home. I'm sure there are many more tips to make the trip easier. I'll close with another entry from my mom:

Finally, I have to keep reminding myself that I am not alone. Neither are you! This is something I say to myself, out loud, and then I say it again. I am not alone. God is in this with me! He is in this for you. We can cry out to Him and He will listen. I try not to sputter or fume about the happenings of the day. After all, He is God. He is in control.

"Shh, My child. Now really, is this what you were crying out to Me about? Quiet now, for I am here with you. Can you stand up? There! Now, take My hand and let's climb out of here." So, He pulls, and I hang on for dear life. Then we talk. Oh true, I mumble and grumble, but I have concluded that God will never let me go. He hushes my whining and listens to what I have to say.

Goodness, this has all the earmarks of the sermon of the century, does it not? But honestly, God is in the driver's seat. God has thought this age-thing through. Remember that old man called Caleb? He was that spy way back in the Old Testament. You remember—Joshua and Caleb. Did Caleb run out of gas? Not once. Listen to Caleb talking:

> *Now then, just as the LORD promised,*
> *he has kept me alive for forty-five years*
> *since the time he said this to Moses,*
> *while Israel moved about in the wilderness.*

In Times Like These ...

So here I am today, eighty-five years old!
I am still as strong today
as the day Moses sent me out;
I'm just as vigorous to go out to battle now
as I was then.
Joshua 14:10-11 NIV

Lord, this day please give us Caleb-confidence! Grant
us patience, dear Lord, for today and all the todays that might
follow. ~ Mildred Krentel

Thank you

. . . to my husband for his "ever-ready," loving encouragement to keep at it to the end to see the God- stories in the events we weathered together through our 52 years get into print.

. . . my mother for inspiring me with her example to write down my stories.

. . . and my editor and publisher, Marlene Bagnull, for her never-ending determination to get it right—right down to crossing every "t" and dotting every "I." She has been my caring prayer partner over the Internet and my faithful cheerleader and teacher.

Made in the USA
Middletown, DE
23 December 2020